NEWSMAKERS

STEVE JOBS

Visionary Founder of Apple

by Marylou Morano Kjelle

Content Consultant
Anthony Rotolo, Professor
S. I. Newhouse School of Public Communications
Syracuse University

Core Library

An Imprint of Abdo Publishing
www.abdopublishing.com

www.abdopublishing.com

Published by Abdo Publishing, a division of ABDO, PO Box 398166, Minneapolis, Minnesota 55439. Copyright © 2015 by Abdo Consulting Group, Inc. International copyrights reserved in all countries. No part of this book may be reproduced in any form without written permission from the publisher. Core Library™ is a trademark and logo of Abdo Publishing.

Printed in the United States of America, North Mankato, Minnesota
082014
012015

Cover Photo: Paul Sakuma/AP Images
Interior Photos: Paul Sakuma/AP Images, 1, 29, 34; Beck Diefenbach/Reuters/Corbis, 4; Jeff Chiu/AP Images, 7, 45; Seth Poppel/Yearbook Library, 10; Kimberly White/ Corbis, 13; Red Line Editorial, 16; Roger Ressmeyer/Corbis, 18; Michael Hicks, 21 (top); Apple/AP Images, 21 (bottom), 22, 26; Brant Ward/San Francisco Chronicle/ Corbis, 31; Susan Ragan/Reuters/Corbis, 37; Anthony Behar/Sipa Press/AP Images, 40

Editor: Arnold Ringstad
Series Designer: Becky Daum

Library of Congress Control Number: 2014944215

Cataloging-in-Publication Data
Kjelle, Marylou Morano.
 Steve Jobs: visionary founder of Apple / Marylou Morano Kjelle.
  p. cm. -- (Newsmakers)
Includes bibliographical references and index.
ISBN 978-1-62403-642-2
1. Jobs, Steve, 1955-2011--Juvenile literature. 2. Computer engineers--United States-
-Biography--Juvenile literature. 3. Businessmen--United States--Biography--Juvenile
literature. 4. Apple Computer, Inc.--History--Juvenile literature.   1.Title.
338.7/61004092--dc23
[B]

2014944215

CONTENTS

CHAPTER ONE

THE YEAR OF THE IPAD 2

The audience cheered as Steve Jobs took the stage at the Yerba Buena Center for the Arts in San Francisco, California. It was March 2, 2011. Many people in the audience were surprised to see him. Jobs had been battling pancreatic cancer for several years. He was on sick leave from his position as the chief executive officer (CEO) of Apple Inc. He had founded the company in 1976. Now, Jobs looked

Jobs was famous for his onstage product announcements.

frail but also excited. He stood onstage wearing his usual black shirt, jeans, and running shoes. He had come to launch Apple's newest product, the iPad 2.

The iPad 2 is a tablet. Tablets are flat, rectangular computers. People interact with them using large touchscreens. The devices can run games, play music, browse the Internet, and run all kinds of programs.

Before talking about the iPad 2, Jobs updated the audience on its predecessor. The first iPad had been hugely successful. More than 15 million were sold. Jobs called it the most successful consumer product in history.

What's in a Name?

The computer company Jobs founded in 1976 needed a name. Jobs was on an all-fruit diet at the time. He had just returned from an apple orchard near Portland, Oregon. He decided Apple would be a fun name for a computer company. Personal computers were a new technology. Some consumers felt they would be too complicated to use. Jobs thought connecting the word *apple* with *computer* would make the machines feel friendlier.

The iPad 2 was released on March 11, nine days after Jobs's presentation.

Jobs predicted the new device would be just as successful. He said 2011 would be remembered as the year of the iPad 2. As it turned out, Jobs did not live to see the end of the year. He died of cancer on October 5, 2011. He was 56 years old.

A Magical and Revolutionary Device

When it released the iPad in 2010, Apple called the tablet a "magical and revolutionary device." Users interact with its large touchscreen using their fingers. A few years earlier, Apple had introduced the iPhone, its first popular touchscreen device. In many ways, the iPad is an enlarged iPhone. Software applications, known as apps, made the iPad a popular device. People have developed hundreds of thousands of apps for the iPad. They range from games to educational programs to social networking tools.

Jobs the Visionary

Jobs was among the greatest technology visionaries of the last century. He helped create the personal computer industry in the 1980s. Decades later, he changed to the music, cell phone, and tablet industries. Under Jobs's leadership, Apple changed how people work, listen to music, watch movies, and use computers.

In 1983 Jobs gave a speech in Aspen, Colorado, about the future of computers. He spoke about the new developments he expected in the near future. In the speech, Jobs explained how he wanted Apple to be at the forefront of these changes:

> Apple's strategy is really simple. What we want to do is we want to put an incredibly great computer in a book that you can carry around with you and learn how to use in 20 minutes. That's what we want to do and we want to do it this decade. And we really want to do it with a radio link in it so you don't have to hook up to anything and you're in communication with all of these larger databases and other computers.
>
> Source: Matthew Panzarin. "Rare Full Recording of 1983 Steve Jobs Speech Reveals Apple Had Been Working on iPad for 27 Years." The Next Web. The Next Web, October 2, 2012. Web. Accessed June 24, 2014.

Back It Up

In this part of the speech, Jobs outlines his vision for the future. Compare Jobs's vision to the reality of the iPad 2, released more than 25 years later. Write a paragraph explaining which predictions were right and which were wrong. Use evidence from the speech and from the rest of Chapter One.

CHAPTER TWO

GROWING UP

Steven Paul Jobs was born in San Francisco, California, on February 24, 1955. He was adopted as an infant by a working-class couple named Paul and Clara Jobs. Paul was a high school dropout who held several jobs while Steve was growing up. Clara was a bookkeeper. They were loving parents to Steve and his younger sister, Patricia. Patricia was adopted when Steve was two years old.

Steve's childhood and school years took place in the midst of major technological changes.

Steve spent part of his childhood in Mountain View, California. Mountain View is near San Francisco and San Jose, California. The area between these cities is known as Silicon Valley. The region became home to many technology companies after the 1950s. It was an exciting place to live during Steve's childhood. Technology was growing by leaps and bounds, and it was happening right in his backyard.

Steve's Biological Family

Steve's birth mother was American and his biological father was Syrian. His parents were not married when he was born. They later married and eventually divorced. As an adult, Jobs tracked down and met his mother. He also learned he had a younger sister, novelist Mona Simpson. Jobs decided not to meet his biological father.

School Years

Steve was a smart child. After the fourth grade, he skipped a grade. Even so, Steve found school boring. He played pranks on his classmates to entertain himself. By the time he got to Homestead High School in Cupertino, California, math and science were his favorite

At Apple presentations over the years, Steve sometimes showed photos of his early days with Steve Wozniak, center, in photo.

subjects. He built radios in his garage. The summer between his freshman and sophomore years, Steve went to work at an electronics company. He added nuts and bolts to devices as they moved down an assembly line.

Silicon Valley

Silicon Valley gets its name from the chemical element silicon. Silicon is a semiconductor, a material that conducts electricity in useful ways. Semiconductors are used to create computer chips. In 1971, author Don Hoefler referred to the Santa Clara Valley in California as "Silicon Valley" due to the large number of electronics companies located in the area. The nickname stuck. Silicon Valley is commonly considered the technology hub of the United States.

Steve met lifelong friend Steve Wozniak in high school. Wozniak, nicknamed "Woz" by his friends, was five years older than Steve. He was already in college. The two Steves had a lot in common. They were both interested in electronics. They also liked to play pranks on people and listen to music. Steve was fascinated when Woz told him he had built a computer. Woz was the first person Steve met who knew more about electronics than he did.

When Steve graduated high school in 1972 at age 17, he wasn't sure he wanted to go to college. However, his parents had promised his birth mother they would give him a college education. Steve enrolled at Reed College, a small, private college in Portland, Oregon. Before long, Steve found college boring. Instead of going to his classes, he explored the things that interested him. This included spirituality. He read books on Buddhism and Hinduism. He listened to rock music and became a vegetarian. He also spent a lot of time at an apple orchard near Portland. He remained interested in technology. He believed it was another form of art.

Dropping Out

Steve knew Reed College was expensive for his parents. Additionally, he was not enjoying his experience there. In early 1974, Steve dropped out of college and moved back home. However, he still wanted to explore his spirituality. He decided to travel to India. To earn money for the trip, he worked at Atari, one of the first video game companies. By April, he had saved enough money. Steve traveled to Delhi, India. He stayed there for seven months but was

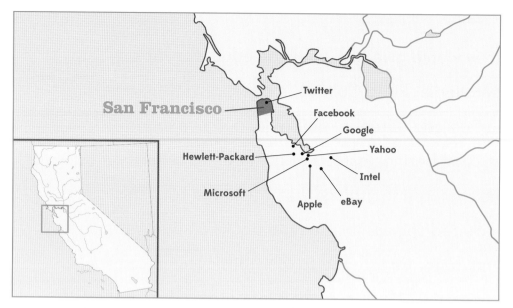

Silicon Valley Map

This map of Silicon Valley shows where several technology companies, including Apple, have headquarters or other large presences. Why do you think so many similar companies are located so near each other? How might nearby San Francisco help to fuel the valley's growth?

unable to find the spiritual answers he was looking for. He returned to California and his job at Atari.

In 1972 Atari had released *Pong*, a table-tennis video game for two players. Nolan Bushnell, Atari's founder, wanted a one-player version of the game. Rather than two players hitting a ball back and forth, one person would hit a ball off a virtual wall. Bushnell challenged Steve to design the circuit board for the new game. To save money, Bushnell wanted to use the least number of computer chips possible.

Steve was not an expert in circuit board designs, so he asked Wozniak to help. He challenged Wozniak to complete the task in four days. This was much quicker than the usual time needed for such a project. Wozniak designed the game, called *Breakout*, and Steve helped build it. They split the $700 payment. Steve didn't tell Wozniak that Atari had offered a bonus based on how few computer chips were used. Steve kept the entire bonus.

CHAPTER THREE

THE BIRTH OF APPLE

n 1975 Wozniak worked at technology company Hewlett-Packard. He was also designing a computer in his spare time. In earlier decades, computers could be the size of entire rooms. Now, new technology allowed them to be made much smaller and cheaper. By June 1975, Wozniak was ready to test his machine. Unlike most computers of the time, it could work with a screen. Other

Wozniak was an avid video game player and began building his own electronic devices.

computers used printouts or rows of lights to display results. Wozniak typed a letter on the keyboard and it showed up on a monitor.

Jobs was impressed by the computer. Wozniak wanted to freely give his design to anyone who wanted to build the computer. However, Jobs thought it would be better for them to build and sell the circuit boards. Jobs convinced Wozniak that they should start their own business. On April 1, 1976 they formed Apple Computer Inc. Their first order for 50 computers came from a local electronics store. The computer, called the Apple I, was sold as a circuit

Computers Then and Now

The top image shows an original Apple I computer in its display case at the Computer History Museum in Mountain View, California. Below it are modern Apple computers. Based on the images and what you've read about these computers, what do they have in common? What is different?

Apple went on to sell millions of Apple II computers.

board. Customers were responsible for adding cases, keyboards, and monitors.

Each partner brought something different to Apple. Wozniak was a talented engineer, so he designed the computers. Jobs was a skilled marketer and leader. He oversaw sales and product development. Their personalities were vastly different. Wozniak was shy. Jobs was forceful and often emotional. The combination worked. The company sold more than 100 computers. This set the stage for Apple's next move.

The Apple II

In 1977 Apple released an updated version of its first computer. The new machine was called the Apple II. It came in a plastic case and featured a built-in keyboard. Even more exciting, the Apple II had color graphics. Soon after the computer's release, a disk drive was created. This enabled users to purchase and use a wide assortment of programs.

Seeing into the Future

The company Xerox is best known for its photocopying machines. But beginning in the 1970s, it also operated a research laboratory at Stanford University in Palo Alto, California. The lab was called the Palo Alto Research Center, or Xerox PARC for short. In 1979 Xerox agreed to allow Jobs and his team to tour the facility. There Jobs saw a computer that used a graphical user interface (GUI). At the time, most computers simply displayed text. A GUI displayed icons, images, and other graphics. Users could navigate the system using a mouse. In 1979 Xerox PARC's ideas were revolutionary. Jobs's team began developing a new computer that used a GUI.

The demand for personal computers grew, and so did Apple. Jobs was only 22 years old when the Apple II was released. He did not have the business experience to run the fast-growing company. Michael Scott joined Apple as CEO to handle the day-to-day business of the company. Jobs became the chairman of Apple's board of directors. He began searching for the next trend in personal computers. Jobs visited a computer research laboratory at nearby Stanford University. He hoped to gather ideas for future Apple products. At the laboratory, he learned about graphical user interfaces. This was a new, easier way to interact with computers. Some people believed it could open up the industry to a mass audience. In a few years, Jobs would use the technology to revolutionize the personal computer industry.

FURTHER EVIDENCE

This chapter includes information about the early years of Apple Computer Inc. What was one of the chapter's main points? What key evidence supports this point? Take a look at the article on the website below. It features some of Steve Wozniak's memories about this time period. Does his account support the main points in the chapter? Write a few sentences using new information from the website as evidence to support a point in the chapter.

Apple: The Early Years
www.mycorelibrary.com/steve-jobs

CHAPTER FOUR

THE NEXT STEP

n 1984 Apple released a new computer called
the Macintosh. It incorporated the technology
Jobs had learned about at Xerox PARC, including
a GUI. But the computer's innovation went further
than its technology. It was also the most stylish
and user-friendly computer of its time. A famous
commercial shown during the 1984 Super Bowl
brought the Macintosh to the public's attention.

The Macintosh's use of a GUI made it more accessible than
previous computers.

Steve Wozniak

Steve Wozniak left Apple in 1985. He returned to college and earned a degree in computer science. He turned his attention toward computer education for both children and adults. Wozniak also helped fund the Electronic Frontier Foundation. This is a nonprofit organization that works to protect the rights of people who use technology. He was also a founding sponsor of the Tech Museum of Innovation in San Jose. In 2006 Wozniak published his autobiography, *iWoz: From Computer Geek to Cult Icon*.

The new machine had drawbacks, however. It ran slower than its competitors. It also had limited memory.

Apple's rise in the computer industry was due in part to Jobs's energy and charisma. He was a skilled motivator. He could also be obnoxious, rude, and selfish. Jobs often behaved as though rules didn't apply to him. He liked to go barefoot, even to important meetings. He occasionally cried when he couldn't have his way. Still, he was amazingly charismatic and persuasive. One Apple employee said Jobs created a "reality distortion field" around him.

Jobs was a skilled and persuasive leader and salesman.

He could make people believe or do anything, even if it seemed outlandish or impossible. He challenged his employees to excel. Jobs demanded that the Macintosh's circuit boards be elegantly designed, even though users would never see them.

By 1985 Jobs had started to clash with Apple's then-CEO, John Sculley. The board members sided with Sculley. They did not formally fire Jobs, but they took away the projects he was working on. They also reduced his responsibilities with the company. Jobs became powerless at the company

Pixar

Jobs made a major career move shortly after his departure from Apple. In 1986 he invested $10 million in the computer graphics company Pixar. Jobs believed computer graphics were the future of animated films. Pixar's first full-length film, *Toy Story*, was released in 1995. It became the highest earning film of the year. It earned more than $550 million. Pixar later released *A Bug's Life*, *Toy Story 2*, *Finding Nemo*, and other popular films. In 2006 the Walt Disney Company bought Pixar for $7.6 billion.

Jobs announced the NeXT computer onstage in San Francisco in March 1989.

he had cofounded less than a decade earlier. Finally, on September 17, 1985, Jobs officially resigned from Apple.

NeXT Inc.

Jobs did not stay idle for long. In 1985 he launched his next computer venture, a company called NeXT Inc. The company created computers for universities and businesses. It also developed an innovative operating system called NeXTSTEP. The operating system was exclusively available on NeXT's computers. However, the company was unsuccessful. At $6,500, its first computer was extremely expensive. The company began focusing on software rather than hardware. It worked on its operating system and other programs rather than designing and building computers. In 1992 Jobs decided to license the NeXTSTEP operating system to other computer manufacturers.

Meanwhile, Apple was also having problems. At first the company had done well after Jobs's departure. In the early 1990s, however, Apple began losing business to competitors. Microsoft, a software company founded by Bill Gates in 1975, introduced new versions of its own operating system. The operating system was called Windows. It became extremely popular, but it was incompatible with Apple's computers. Apple needed a new, modern operating system to compete. NeXT needed the help of a major company to support its software. Apple made a decision that laid the foundation for Jobs's comeback. In 1996 Apple purchased NeXT for more than $400 million. Jobs became Apple's interim CEO.

CHAPTER FIVE

THE RETURN

With Jobs back, Apple was on track to becoming a strong company again. Jobs focused the company's efforts. He shut down many projects that had been initiated after his departure. In 1998 Apple released a successful new computer called the iMac. Its colorful case was a major departure from the beige boxes of most personal computers. Jobs dropped the "interim" from

The iMac helped reinvigorate Apple following Jobs's return.

iPods

When they were first released, iPods were only compatible with Apple's computers. This limited the devices' potential. Only a small percentage of consumers owned computers made by Apple. In 2002 Apple released an iPod compatible with Windows. Sales exploded. Eventually Apple controlled more than 90 percent of the digital music player market.

his job title in 2000. The next year, a new Apple product would bring massive changes to the music industry.

In October 2001, Jobs announced a portable music player called the iPod. It had a tiny, high-capacity hard drive. It could hold hundreds of songs. The iPod became enormously popular. In 2003 Apple announced the iTunes Music Store. This online marketplace allowed people to easily buy music online. Before, customers had to purchase an entire album even if they wanted just one song. Now they could buy individual songs and load them onto their iPods. The store sold millions of songs. The music industry shifted its focus to take advantage of digital downloads.

The success of the iPod transformed Apple from a computer company to a consumer electronics company.

The Diagnosis

Jobs received frightening news in October 2003. He was diagnosed with pancreatic cancer. Despite the pleas of his family and friends, Jobs refused to have surgery. He underwent alternative treatments, such as acupuncture and special diets. Finally, in July 2004, he agreed to undergo surgery. Jobs had part of his pancreas removed. However, by that time the cancer had spread to his liver. Jobs took a leave of absence from Apple to recover.

When he returned in the fall of 2005, Jobs turned his attention to the iPhone. The new device was finally released in June 2007. The touchscreen and elegant software were popular among consumers. Before the iPhone, touchscreens were relatively rare. Within a few years after the phone's release, nearly all smartphones looked very similar to the iPhone.

In the meantime, Jobs continued to struggle with his health. Still, he did not reveal his cancer diagnosis to the public. In March 2009, Jobs underwent a liver transplant in Memphis, Tennessee. The new liver seemed to help. After healing in the spring and summer, Jobs enthusiastically returned to work. In the next two years he unveiled the iPad and its successor, the iPad 2. The tablets became two of Apple's most popular products.

However, Jobs's health began to fail again. He announced another period of medical leave in 2011. On August 24, he resigned as Apple's CEO. In a statement, Jobs said he believed that Apple's best days were still to come. He said he looked forward to contributing

The Evolution of the iPhone

Apple has released at least one new version of the iPhone every year since 2007. Updated models included faster processors, more memory, and larger screens. At the same time, Apple has updated the operating system that runs on the iPhone, called iOS. Newer versions introduced updated designs and better performance. By early 2014, the company had sold more than 500 million iPhones.

Apple fans created memorials to Jobs at Apple stores around the world after his death.

to the company in a new way. Less than two months later, Jobs died at his home in Palo Alto, California.

Changing Lives

Steve Jobs changed our digital lives in many ways. Virtually all computers today use the graphical user interfaces he made popular. Millions of people use iPods to listen to music. The development of easy-to-use touchscreens made computers more accessible than ever before. Jobs's vision and strong personality made these advances possible.

In 2008 an editor at *Fortune* magazine interviewed Jobs about the iPhone. Jobs spoke about Apple's decision to produce its own device and enter the smartphone market:

> *We all had cellphones. We just hated them, they were so awful to use. The software was terrible. The hardware wasn't very good. We talked to our friends, and they all hated their cellphones too. Everybody seemed to hate their phones. And we saw that these things really could become much more powerful and interesting to license. It's a huge market. I mean a billion phones get shipped every year, and that's almost an order of magnitude greater than the number of music players. It's four times the number of PCs that ship every year.*
>
> Source: Betsy Morris. "Steve Jobs Speaks Out." CNN Money. CNN, March 7, 2008. Web. Accessed June 24, 2014.

What's the Big Idea?

Take a close look at Jobs's answer. What was Apple's reasoning behind creating a new type of cell phone? Pick out two details that he mentions. What does his answer say about Apple's process for selecting new products to create?

IMPORTANT DATES

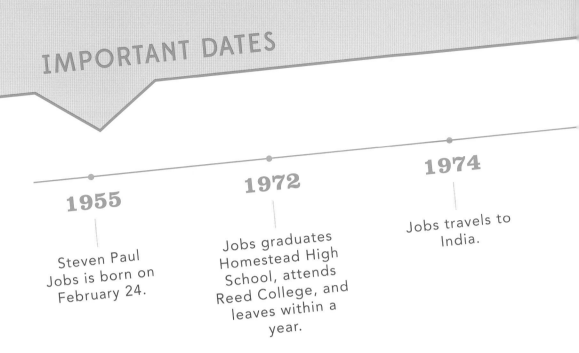

1955

Steven Paul Jobs is born on February 24.

1972

Jobs graduates Homestead High School, attends Reed College, and leaves within a year.

1974

Jobs travels to India.

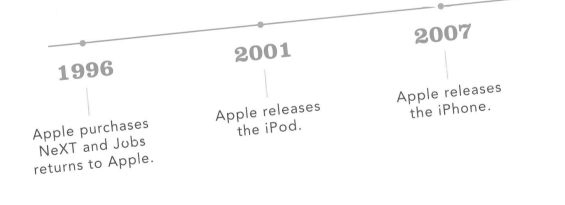

1996

Apple purchases NeXT and Jobs returns to Apple.

2001

Apple releases the iPod.

2007

Apple releases the iPhone.

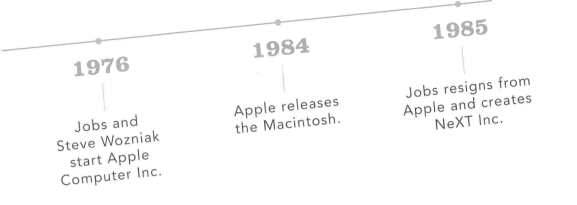

1976

Jobs and
Steve Wozniak
start Apple
Computer Inc.

1984

Apple releases
the Macintosh.

1985

Jobs resigns from
Apple and creates
NeXT Inc.

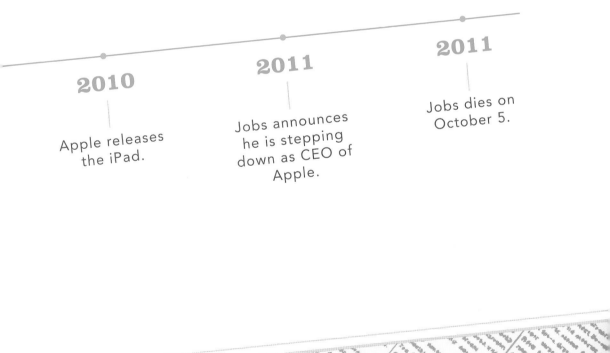

2010

Apple releases
the iPad.

2011

Jobs announces
he is stepping
down as CEO of
Apple.

2011

Jobs dies on
October 5.

Take a Stand

This book discusses Steve Jobs's return to Apple in the 1990s. With an adult's help, search the Internet for articles that discuss this time period in Apple's history and Jobs's life. Imagine you are making the decision for Apple about whether to bring Jobs back to the company. Write a paragraph arguing your opinion on the issue. Support your argument with evidence from this book and the articles you have read.

Tell the Tale

Chapter Three talks about graphical user interfaces. Imagine you are a kid in 1984 and you have just gotten a new Macintosh. Write a few paragraphs that tell the story of how you explain a graphical user interface to your parents. How do you explain concepts like windows, folders, and a mouse?

Say What?

The computer field contains many technical terms. Find five words in this book that you've never heard before. Use a dictionary to find out what they mean. Then write the meanings in your own words, and use each word in a new sentence.

Why Do I Care?

Humans lived for thousands of years without computers. Now it seems as though we can't live without them. Think of a few activities that are routinely done today by computers. How would you do these activities today without a computer?

GLOSSARY

board of directors
a group of people who provide advice to a company's leaders

chairman
the most powerful person on a corporation's board of directors

charisma
special charm or public appeal

chief executive officer (CEO)
the leader of a company

circuit board
the material to which a computer's microprocessor and other chips are attached

innovation
a new method, idea, or device

interim
temporary

operating system
software that controls the operation of a computer and directs the processing of the user's programs

processor
the microchip inside a computer that performs calculations

LEARN MORE

Books

Gregory, Josh. *Steve Jobs.* New York: Scholastic, 2013.

Pollack, Pam. *Who Was Steve Jobs?* New York: Grosset & Dunlap, 2012.

Ziller, Amanda. *Steve Jobs: American Genius.* New York: Collins, 2012.

Websites

To learn more about Newsmakers, visit **booklinks.abdopublishing.com.** These links are routinely monitored and updated to provide the most current information available.

Visit **www.mycorelibrary.com** for free additional tools for teachers and students.

INDEX

ABOUT THE AUTHOR

Marylou Morano Kjelle is a college professor, a freelance writer, and the author of more than 50 books for young people. Many of the books she has written are biographies.